THE KEY CLUB

"Which Daddy is yours, honey?"

Donna Emerich

This is dedicated to Aunt Rose.

Thank you for ALL

The fantastic stories!

Three Belles Publishing

2/14/2025

This book is a work of fiction. Names, characters, businesses, organizations, place, events, and incidents are either a product of the author's imagination or are used fictitiously. Any resemblance to actual people living, dead, or otherwise, events or locales are entirely coincidental.

This book is protected under the copywrite laws of the United States of America. Any reproduction or unauthorized use of the material or artwork contained herein is prohibited without the express written permission of the author.

Prologue

A very long time ago, small towns had a population control problem, without enough people there would be inbreeding. Always families with money had the most lucrative jobs and best properties. While farmers had large families running with many children to lighten the workload.

Shop proprietors were the middle class between the prosperous and lower-class workers. Winters were hard with several feet of snow falling a few times a month. Which made for a boring social life.

During the November meeting of the town board, a discussion was brought forth concerning the lack of births in the tri-county area. "Now do we encourage procreation sex to increase our towns population?"

Judge Herald Began. There had been an upturn in both separation and divorce proceedings through his court room.

Council woman Judith Summers admitted, "**Sex was lacking** in most marriages. But most women did look at farm hands with lusty eyes" Reverand Thomas shook his head and spoke loudly, "This is an abomination in the eyes of our lord!"

Judge Herald announced, "Do you have any have any other suggestions on how to increase our population for the town?" Speaking with all the authority bestowed upon him by the church, "The way God intended as a holy union between husband and wife."

Another voice chimes in, the school principal, Lawrence Sikes explained, "School's are having to close during deer season so the boys can help provide food for their families for the winter." Sherrif Cutter bellows, "The **kids** with too much time on there hands causes **me** problems!"

"Men are running moonshine or drugs to keep their families fed. I can't keep the doctor's office from getting broken into anymore. Plus, the idiots who don't have a drivers license are driving tractors to the saloon. Tractor tickets don't bring in much revenue."

Bill Emerson, highway super intendant, explains "The VFW still gets a good crowd on the weekend, but our teenagers steal the salt meant for our roads for their own amusement." Frank and Roseline, who owns the local bowling alley and café, explains "We thought of making League teams for family entertainment."

Lily who runs the local beauty parlor and trade school smiled as she spoke, "There are other ways to *stimulate* interests!" The Reverend roared in anger, "No Brothels!" Shaking his head Judge Herald slammed down his gavel, "Look! We need to increase our tri-county population. So, we've come up with a plan,"

Continuing, Judge Herald explains, "This Has to be voluntary. We will send out invitations to the first meeting of the **Key Club**"

Confused Bill asked council woman Judith Summers, "Is this like cheating on your woman?" "No, everyone will have to agree to the rules of the club," Judith replied, "It will all be explained at the first meeting. Good night, Bill." As Judith drove home, her thoughts wandered towards the key club.

Thinking about the many classes of people with lineage that goes back centuries. Social classes in small towns don't mix so the key club will need to be a club for exclusivity.

That way when pregnancies do happen the blood mixing will produce pure children. Thinking aloud, "I'll have to put feelers out in the social clubs. May be find out what the other women find attractive in their men. Qualities that are good for breeding. The process should look anonymous, keys in a bowl, so no one feels left out."

Judith screams, "This is not a scientific experiment! We need children for the town to survive!" As Judith pulls into a darkened driveway, she knew nothing awaited her except a dark house with her sleeping spouse. Her children sneak into the kitchen for a bedtime snack. "Goodnight mom!"

As Judith crept into bed she reached for her husband Jack Summers. Next thing she knows she feels his strong arms wrapping around her. Jack whispers, "Did you get them all fired up?" Judith smiles and explains, "Yes, it's all set up, first meeting is a week from Thursday. Invitations will be sent out to see who bites." Jack sneers, "They have no idea what this is all about do they?" "Increasing the population Jack," replied Judith.

Laughing heartily, "So they say" snapped Jack. "But I know that devious mind of yours." Cackled Jack. "Now, give me some before I have to share you."

As the beauty shop buzzed with news of the town board meeting, ladies of the church were appalled... Or were they? Many skeletons in those closets hiding under the perfectly folded linens. Not even bleach could cover the smell of disdain in a so-called perfect place.

Positive the reverend would address the meeting at this Sunday's service. Our ladies of the church promise not to entertain gossip on Lord's Day. Lilly thought, *but in small gatherings there is not much else to do.* She took a long pull off her cigarette remembering how many shotgun weddings took place in a town of such perfect people.

Smiling to herself Lilly cackled, *even Reverend Thomas has had some wrinkles in his fine collar of starched white. He's been known to partake in things he so vigilantly preaches against.* Lilly sighs *then there's the young men and women who have come home after serving their country to a town full of strangers, who don't remember their names.*

The whispers of mental defects caused during an act of war against our own. Lilly knows secret trysts out of town visiting families. The visits clouded by the sanitarium or a hospital to have conditions cleaned deep from the injured soul. A body will heal but the soul needs forgiveness for reasons unknown.

As Lilly headed back to her house of beauty, she shook her head knowing the only beauty at the end of her day was a fatter bank account and the ice clinking as scotch poured with diligence awaiting her lips.

The shop was unusually busy for the middle of the week, but news spreads faster than wildfire here in our country. Even men are coming in for services since our local barber has closed for a vacation. Seems he has a sick family member, but everyone knows his daughter had a breakdown.

As dusk sets in the last of the chores are being done. With supper on the stove for most of the town's folk. After the children headed to bed, parents spoke softly of the club. Many wanted no part of such a devious plot by the town board. Others admitted curiosity had gotten better of them.

Questions:

1.) How would the rules be enforced?

2.) Who made the rules?

3.) How much are you required to participate? Or can you just watch?

4.) Will the club break up marriages?

The buzz in town was deafening. Meanwhile Frank and Roselyn were discussing options of events to be held by the club for adults to enjoy. Roz explains to Frank, "Summer can be BBQ's, camping, and outdoor parties. Winters are sleighrides, bowling, country club weekend dances, and card games." Frank pouted,

"How do we keep guys from bragging and such?" Roz scratches her head, "Guess that should be laid out in the rules."

Frank explains, "I feel like there needs to be some anonymity in place otherwise marriages would crumble." Roz spoke softly, "Feelings could be hurt and hearts broken so I guess that's why a private club would be the best option." Frank cracked, "Technically we would be considered swingers. What about the children though?" Roz quipped, "I guess they would all be raised together as they are now. Same school activities. But what about diseases?" she asked.

Rubbing his chin Frank said, "I guess we need to get a doctor on board with our club." Roz looked confused, "Where are we going to find a doctor that is going to be willing?"

"Brothels, or Gentlemen's clubs all keep a doctor on staff. I see no reason we couldn't have one either. We'll have to check around."

Roz rubbed Frank's shoulders, "This is more complicated than we thought." "Guess so, nothing is set in stone, just ideas." "So, who's on your lust list Frank?" questioned Roz.

"Just you dear." Frank smiled. "That's bullshit, but thanks for the confidence boost!" Roz laughed. "Oh, inventory start in the morning, so we'd better head off to bed. Trucks roll in at 6am." Growling Frank said, "Christ! Look outside, possible snow day. It's a good time for deer hunting, especially for the newbies." Giggled Frank. "Fresh snow is always soft Roz, how 'bout it?" Turning Frank saw Roz was sleeping, hugging her pillow tightly.

Starting out the door, watching the snow cover the front lawn, and the parking lot next door, Frank knew he would not rest. Dressing quietly, Frank headed over to the bowling alley to start the coffee and inventory. Snowplows would be on the road shortly. At 6am school closings started to be announced.

Kids standing next to the radio, fingers crossed, hoping their school would be closed. It wasn't often they got lucky enough to have a snow day. The schools believed in chained tires. Families in the back hills came in on tractors and horse pulled wagons. As news of the club idea spread to other parts of the tri-county area. All watching to see if the idea would come to fruition or just remain an idea that would be smashed down by the local churches.

As Sunday came around, Reverend Thomas preached how anyone who entertained the idea of the club would burn in hell for eternity. The nodding of the congregation pushed the Reverend into screaming, fists shaking, a moral man who was barely hanging on to his church. Passing the plate got very little in the way of money for the church.

Reverend Thomas had ambitions of a larger church, with massive stained-glass windows, a house of his own that was separate from the parsonage. A permanent home, no more shuffling from church to church. His only advantage to being shuffled around from church to church was a larger dating pool.

The reverend never had an empty fridge, or lack of dinner invitations. Those ripe innocent girls looking for spiritual guidance. Thomas thought, *oh shit, I am beginning to sweat how unbecoming. I need to keep my composure.*

As you look inside our small town, we are a loving supportive community, but as you look closer, there is more than meets the eye. Never take your eye off the prize! The children to have heard of the adults only club, in their eyes the less parental supervision, the more fun for them to have. Parents mean rules, no fun.

The church auxiliary meeting opened its meeting by covering the holiday bake sale, and the Christmas story tryouts for this year. Basically, it's a popularity contest so parents can show off their progeny. New business came in with, if you choose to be a part of the club then you are no longer welcome in the church auxiliary events.

"How can you demand we choose when the club hasn't been officially started yet?" "We don't even know if it will be a private club." "So, what's the deal Judith?"

"We have sent invitations to anyone who we thought would be interested, and just like any other organized club, there will be rules. Maybe even dues or fund raising for events." "It sounds ungodly to me," growled another woman. "It sounds like you have made up your minds without hearing the idea out." Retorted Judith.

Mumbling spread between those gathered. Judith knew she hit a nerve. "Now any other **real** church business?" The alderman meeting covered the same issues, but with a slightly different twist. "Is it like whatever happens at these events stays there?" Judge Harold explains, "When you sign up to be in the club, you don't discuss it outside of the club." "What if **our wives** don't want to join? Can we join without them?"

Thinking a moment Judge Harold smiled, "That's a damn good question, I will jot that down and find out!" "Is it like swapping?" "Let's not put the cart before the horse. Let's see who shows up first, it may be a bust. Now," said Frank, "Curiosity will bring them to the meeting, but rules are what will keep them or send them away.

Bill questioned, "Everyone has his or her own reasons to join, but the underlying concerns are lack of population for our farms." "You have to have people to work the farms, the factories, the shops, etc etc."

"People are practicing safe sex, if any sex. Large families are not encouraged anymore. We need to bring them back into sex. Sex out of obligation is a job that *no one* enjoys," whined Frank.

Sherrif Cutter said, "Well this could backfire on us, and have over population." Judge Harold snarked, "Then you will need a bigger budget, won't you?" Cutter retorted, "Kids need to be controlled." "But they are also our next generation," snapped Judge Harold.

"You know that also means more teachers, a bigger school budget Lawrence." "True but how do we teach the boys hunting? Isn't a class skill needed to be practiced daily?"

"With patience, because they are taught from an early age. Hunting is necessary to feed families."

"We're obligated to teach them the difference. Educated students share with their community as teachers, engineers, or factory foreman. All knowledge is important." "Well said Larry," smiled Judge Harold. "What are your thoughts, Bill?" "I'd like to see the kids learn what it takes to keep our highways, and rivers cleaned up. No one appreciates road upkeep until they must use a detour." "Kids don't know how to use rebar or tar to fix surfaces, they just want to sit around!"

"Our kids and the adults need to learn a trade." Laughing Frank announced, "Sounds like we are all on the same page." "What about Reverend Thomas?" "He's a pain, and his closet isn't free of sin, he will fall in line."

"Harold what do you have in mind?" "It's best if you do not know." With the slamming of the gavel the alderman meeting came to an end.

As Judge Harold arrives at his personal chambers, he looks around at all his accolades, pictures with the governors, and congressmen. He drifts back to his first case as a D.A and how much time has passed since he passed the bar.

He was so young, an idealistic attorney, the law was about justice. Harold soon discovered small town politics dictated money & knowledge kept you on the right side of whose ever law was broken. The adage of *Money talks & bullshit walks* will always be true in small town law.

Still, Harold believed in the principal *Innocent until proven guilty*. If you can, afford to pay for your innocence. The glasses of whiskey go down easier these days, along with the guise *it's best for our community*.

Looking at a picture from far away Harold looks at a beautiful wife taken from him too soon. "I'm doing what's right, so I can be with you soon."

A brain aneurism took the light from Hildy's eyes & soul. Her death didn't come easy but long and lingering. In a moment of lucidity Hildy asked Harold, "Please let me go." Knowing he couldn't stand causing her pain,

Harold fixed her a last drink to send her on her way free of pain.

The doctor wrote it up as she died in her sleep. Long before the need to defile a soul for a listed cause of death. She had been dressed to the nines as Hildy was laid to rest.

Harold talks with her each night before bed as he says good night. *So, as I say, there will never be a closet skeleton free.* Holding a small blue bottle, Harold fondles the curves of its sides, *soon Hildy soon.*

Going back behind the desk Harold pulls out a pen, writing paper, and a book on contract law.

An odd combination to say the least as he researched, he began writing his notes. Rules, they needed iron clad rules, with no way to be misinterpreted.

    1.) *Couples only, you sign in with a partner.*

    2.) *No leaving a spouse for sex in the club.*

3.) *All children will be taken care of as a community effort.*

4.) *No family goes without.*

5.) *All members are expected to help when called upon.*

Rubbing his head, he jotted *physicals* before heading to bed. Morning came too early, it was Thursday, and time to count the RSVP's.

Lilly pouted with disappointment as there were only 5 couples, but as the day started ladies would nonchalantly drop envelopes in the lock box. Lilly smiled; *there's hope for this town yet,* thoughts danced in her mind of fun activities to be had by all. Calling to make sure everything for the meeting was a go.

Lilly called Roz; "Roz, it's Lilly, is there anything I can bring for the meeting?" "How many couples?" asked Roz. "25 and counting!" "Okay we will be ready at 7:30pm." Nobody wants to be the first one at the party or meeting in this case. Some of the men bowled a few games, while ladies enjoyed a pop and hors d'oeuvres. As Judge Harold entered the lanes, there was a silent acknowledgement of his presence.

Lilly arrived with flaming red nails, and a leather-bound notebook under her arm. Lilly was flamboyant to say the very least. Her need for heavy machinery rumbling beneath her showed in her collection of cars & trucks. Four cars and three pickup trucks to be exact.

Lilly had been married a few times; she always outlived her newest husband. She acquired men as if they were accessories for her latest fashion. She had once thought of giving birth to a beautiful child but when a doctor told her a heart condition would prove childbirth difficult for her. She chose to end any option of childbirth. Instead, she shared her wealth with all the local children, including the orphanage.

Truth be told she would go out to do hair for the colored children in their homes. Give their parents after hour jobs so they would feel they earned her generosity. Christmas was her favorite time of the year when her generosity would not meet the gaze of the snobs with more than they need. Even the shopkeepers looked down their nose, but never turned away a cash purchase no matter the color of their skin.

Lilly had been looked upon as a trashy woman, but truth be known she was honest, fair, and willing to help with money, job, or food left at someone door. Lilly enjoyed the company of men but kept her hands off married men. She knew the value of her time and wouldn't waste it with a married man.

As the couple's started to head into the meeting, Lilly greeted everyone with a big smile. As the meeting was brought to order, Harold started explaining the key club.

Charter Rules:

1. This is an adult club.
2. Couples only.
3. What happens in Key Club events stays there.
4. There's no bullshit of dissolving marriages. If anything, husbands may try harder with their wives, as wives may be more affectionate with their spouses.
5. Everyone submits regular physical exams to rule out any medical conditions.
6. Absolutely no rubbing things in your spouse's face, you will be removed.

7. This is a private club! Not just anyone can join. Membership drives are once a year.

8. If any children are conceived, they will be raised in a community family setting. The children will belong to all members.

9. We promote charity and assistance to all participating parties.

10. Your being in this club has no bearing on your religious affiliation. Keep them separate.

11. Dues are paid once a month toward funding events. $2.00 per person.

If this is acceptable, sign up and we'll get physicals set up. "Question Harold, how does this work? Once we have been through the signup and physicals." "We'll start the next club meeting with how this will all work.

Forms are to be signed and given to Lilly." As the buzz between couples got loud, Roz offered refreshments to sooth feathers.

Bill asked, "So, Harold, how many do you think will stay?" "Some will wrestle with their conscience and some it will be a walk on the wild side. Now we wait." "So who's the gate keeper?"

"I guess the members of the town board that are here. It will take time but once started it will run on its own." "But bragging will be an issue." "Not necessarily because these couples will still have their normal jobs, not something discussed for public scrutiny." "What about gays?" Harold laughed, "That's a whole different club."

"Lilly doesn't have a spouse," complained Bill. Harold laughs, "She's to much woman for most of us." "So, we will put her in charge of recruitment." "Is she a Madame?" asked

Larry. Using his authoritative tone, Harold said, "No, but she's very well connected. Politicians consult with her for advice."

"Nice," cackled Larry. "It's better to have her on your side," smiled Harold.

Bill cracked, "She'd make a powerful enemy." "I agree," quipped the Judge. "So, Lilly, how did we do?" "Call doctor Halloway to see who has an updated physical on file, and who needs one done. All 25 couples signed on." "How do we ease them into things?" asked Harold. Lilly smiled, "With both feet Harold."

"Come on Lil." "Well, I thought that on the first night everyone gets a special pretty key to represent being a member. Then we have a type of party at a hotel or designated spot with drinks and dancing." "All couples put their room keys/car keys in a bowl and at the end of the evening reach into the bowl, grab a set of keys, then you go with said owner of the keys." "We should try an overnight first, then graduate to a weekend event."

"Excuses for the family is simple, we had too much to drink and decided to get a room for the night. It's simple. Then with each event they get a little bolder." "Each person has their own preferences, so those will have to be explored as well." "Sounds like Lilly has it all figured out," smirked Sheriff Cutter. "No David, but it needs to be carefully handled." "Secrets can be harmful, like voyeurism." "Got ya Lilly. You understand discretion." "More than you know," snapped Lilly.

Larry says, "Guess even our rock tough sheriff has secrets." "We all do," chimed Bill. "Okey, we started the ball rolling let's head out."

Dr. Halloway scheduled physicals, making notes on heart issues, impotence issues, diabetes, and any other problems that could be passed on in pregnancy.

While going through his notes Dr. Dale Halloway Jr. looked to a picture of his dad holding his medical degree with pride for his son.

"Dad, I never thought I would be getting paid for such an odd request. Is this what being a rural doctor is about? I miss the city, just straight doctoring. No small-town politics, or who owes who. I miss you dad."

As nurse Kelly knocked, she realized she startled her boss. "It's ok, I talk to my dad a lot these days" Nurse Kelly smiled, "Don't forget school physicals for the wrestling team and rifling club." "I have it written down; I won't be late." "The coach wanted me to remind you." "Set up the urine sample kits please. The boys are mandated for testing." "I hear there's girls trying out for the rifle club this year." Smiled Kelly.

"If they want to make the team, they'd better be an excellent marksman. Most of their male counter parts were raised with a gun by the age of 5."

"There must be good Marine recruiters smishing up to them!" "Good Lord Kelly." "Well otherwise they are just going to be slotted up for female jobs and diaper duty." "The militaries are slotted for career advancement for women." "Doctor Halloway, you sound pro female." "You sound surprised, my sister is a major in the army nurse corps. It was the only way; she was not judged for being single in our hometown. So, anything that gives women a leg up career wise is good."

"I started out in microbiology," stated Kelly, "Then transferred to the nursing program." "Males dominated the academy?" questioned Halloway. "Exactly," snapped nurse Kelly.

"Now that you have enlightened me on our lacking education system, back to work." Crack Dr. Halloway.

By the end of the day Dale headed home to his dad's house. Along with his medical practice, Jr. received 50,000 in stocks and the family home. As he entered, Dale felt an ice-cold grip on his arm. He always referred to it as his dad's embrace. Senior was never much on praise, promotion, or affection. What was expected was done with no questions asked.

Perfection at all costs, nothing less was acceptable. Walking through the house, Dale was reminded of the lady who died giving him life. His father never forgave him or let him forget it. The only female influences in his life were housekeeping and nannies. A doctor's life is dedicated, solitude, and service. As Dale climbs the stairs, he feels another cold chill and says, "Love you mom, goodnight."

Judge Harold sits reviewing the medical files, and decides they are ready for meeting number 2. The general buzz in town was that the private club was a go. Sexual perversions are acceptable but never talked about. Most people have lines they won't cross. Most want to try things they have heard about. A slap and tickle, cross dressing maybe, some silk ties. Nothing to rough.

As a thought crossed Harold's mind, *what would be punishment for crossing the lines and how much is too much. These couples are willing so that tells me they are ready for fun.* A buzzing sound shook Judge Harold from his thoughts. "Sir, Lilly is here, she's on her break." "Send her in"

Lilly came bouncing through the door with the vigor of a lioness pup. "So medical files turned out ok. Just the normal heart, diabetes, impotence. But nothing to translate in utero." "If population is important then we should try to plan for cycles."

Cracked Lilly. Thinking a moment, Harold says, "If we make it clinical couples won't enjoy themselves." "Events need to be fun and inviting, so more will want to join the club. The more people, the more variety of participants, the better the chance of babies arriving." "Harold, this is the human part of the equation. Happy humans hump." Laughing Harold says, "I agree."

"So next meeting we will go out to drink & dance. Does next Friday sound workable?" "Yes, I will start looking for a motel with a bar nearby." "Easy does it judge; take it slow the first few times. This is new to these people." "Yes, I understand that, Lilly." "I was feeling out the ladies, some are really excited at the prospects of fun without repercussions." "The men are apprehensive, afraid it will backfire on them." "I see," smiled Lilly. "I'm sure after the first few times they will relax a bit."

"Keep me informed," requested Harold. "Don't I always?" chimed Lilly.

Bill had checked into group rates at resort areas. Local and tri-county. Reviewing the list, he realized dues would need to increase substantially. They just need to get started to attract more couples.

Lawrence was figuring out how to get more from the schoolrooms, for extra students. The whole plan was in motion! Reserving the whole 3rd floor of a local establishment didn't require a major explanation surprisingly.

Judge Harold took money from his discretionary fund for the Key Club meeting. He would advise the town board before the next meeting. Knowing the town may have to cover the first few events. He even anticipated having to use personal funds in leu of having to answer to the board and Reverend Thomas.

Friday night would be filled with drinks and dancing for the couples of the key club.

Lilly passed out news through her salon. Babysitters would be needed as parents would be out having fun. Frank & Roselyn passed plates around to their children, discussing events at school. Frank Jr. spoke, "So, is the key club going to be like the ones in high school?" Choking on his meat Frank said, "Excuse me?" "Key clubs are exclusive to kids that have good grades, practice charity, and good moral character."

Taking in a large breath Roselyn said, "Yes, it's a private club with invitations sent out to our best citizens in town." Frank Jr. said, "So it's exclusive?" "Yes, once it's up and running I'm sure we will have a membership drive." "Kinda like a fraternity or sorority, only the best." "Exactly, colleges have key clubs. Now finish your supper, homework needs to be done." Roselyn smiled.

Roz wiped her brow, "That was a tough conversation to have." Frank laughed, "Before you know it the kids will think it's like belonging to the VFW or a bowling league." "The exclusive part troubles me, what about diversity?"

"All in time," Frank smiled. "So do we carpool or drive separate to these events?" "Good question. We'll be sure to ask the judge at the next meeting." "There should be more information the closer we get to next Friday. Lilly always seems to know the latest word."

As the final plans were put down the couples that signed up received a pastel peach envelope with the address for the evening's entertainment and accommodations list, including a map to the destination. Couples came into the salon for a freshen up. Hair, nails, and eyebrows. Men came for a shave, tonic, and to tighten up their pores. Each couple received a key to prove membership status.

The design was that of an old skeleton key, ornate, with carved flowers for the ladies. The men received a plain key hard, hard stiff material, much in the way they were perceived to be. A nervous electricity had started to fill the air. Men took care to puff out their chest to be noticed. Doctor Halloway had received requests for diet pills, pep/energy cause they were tired, and sedatives for trouble sleeping with the ladies.

Doctor Halloway was requested to be on standby just in case. A light scent of lavender, jasmine, and after shave filled the air.

Lilly enjoyed watching the preparations unfold. "You would think the Lord himself was making an appearance to this crowd." "The confessional will be busy on Saturday afternoon." Cackled Lilly.

Reverend Thomas knew of the events coming to pass on Friday. With his hands he could only offer moral guidance when asked.

Thomas's feelings were actually hurt, because he was not invited, nor was his input asked for. He decided to wait for an invitation. They would surely need your expert advice on sin, or at least how to ask for forgiveness.
What does this say to our youth? The need for good morals abstinence before the holy union of marriage.

This shall be the subject of my next sermon....

As time came to crawl, waiting for Friday, the tension was so thick you could cut it with a knife.

Friday finally arrived; Ladies spent their days making casseroles & desserts for their families. The ladies painted up as smoothly as a porcelain doll. Cheeks flushed with a touch of crimson. Eyes wide with wonder.

The husbands concerned who they will end up with, will she be pretty or butt'erfac'd.

Slowly the arrival of cars trickled into the parking lot. At the door each person was asked to show their key upon admittance to the dance hall. Husbands were then asked to sign the hotel registry. Judge Herald had already paid for the rooms. So, no embarrassing questions.

With the arrival of the band, things became relaxed. Waitresses came and gathered drink orders and hors d'oeuvres. As couples started to dance the judge looked on, a smile creeping at the sides. Lilly grabbed Harold by the arm, "How about taking me for a spin around the dance floor." Harold looking into Lilly's twinkling blue eyes. "Don't know if I can keep up with you, Miss Lilly." "I will slow down so you can catch up with me Herold." "Do you have designs on me Miss Lilly?"

"You won't know until I have you roped and tied Sugar." "Very well, Let's dance."

Liquid greased the wheels to an uneasy crowd. Anxiety, excitement, and plain inadequacy filled the air. Lilly guiltily informs the couples, "It's time each man is to throw his room key in the bowl. Each lady is to face straight ahead and walk past the bowl and pluck a key from the bowl. Go to the same room, your partner will join you. 1 person at a time, no discussions."

"We will meet for coffee tomorrow morning at 11a.m. check out time. If there's any questions, Lilly will come around to answer you individually." With apprehension each woman grabbed a room key and headed for their room. Bold men help the lady's hands, walking them to their destinations with pride. Slowly opening the door, the couples began a journey into experiences only felt in lustful dreams.

The men started with a get to know you talk, next came sexual preference, things they've always wanted to try.

Surprising results came from this phase. Seems the men had limited experiences also.

For most men oral sex was something associated with "Bad Girls". Many of the men had not pleasured a woman orally. Apparently it would be a learning process for both parties.

Lilly told the women, "Feel free to try out new positions, explore every part of your partners body, never hold back. Men taste and touch every part of her body." As exploration began, sounds of pleasured moans, and giggling began to fill the air. Lilly laid on her bed listening to the sounds of pleasure singing through the air. As she was about to overcome, there was a soft knock on her door. She opened the door flushed in crimson. Judge Harold asks, "Am I interrupting?" "Of course, not Harold, I was just thinking of you." "As I walked the hallway, I believe couples are getting into the spirit of thin0gs." "So, what are we to do? We are not coupled Harold."

"Are you propositioning me Miss Lilly?" "Propositioning hell, lets show the club how to do it right." Pulling off his tie, Harold smiled.

"I'm ready for my lessons Mis Lilly." As Lilly grabbed Harolds belt, her hand slid firmly around gripping a hand full of buttock pulling him flush against her curvaceous figure. Lilly wasn't a tall woman by any means, but she filled all the places, even at their age her calves were sleek overture of the care she put into her health but her physique as well.

She was fierce, confident, passionate in nearly everything she did. He knew this was going to be one hell of a ride. He was too hard for him to feel guilty. "Any lower with those fingers Miss Lilly and you will find more than bargained for."

Lilly cackles, "Let's hope so," She abruptly turns, Harolds silk tie slithering slowly across his skin as he watches her saunter away, *uuunnnnmm them supple hips.*

Whether he agreed or not, Harold was already following, mesmerized in her sensual spell. Lilly sauntered about the room casually announcing, "I believe this tie looks better on me, Harold."

Her voice a throaty purr as her gaze prowled like a lioness about to pounce upon its prey. She was dangerous, even in bed, Harold licked his lips ready to join the game that was a foot. "Of course it looks better on you, you aren't wearing anything else." Harold stalks the room slowly as his eyes never tear from her. His clothes seeming to appear on the floor one piece at a time. The corners of her mouth quark and a twinkle sparks in her eyes, and he knows she plans fowl. There was a charge in the air that was electric and prickled the skin. It started as a soft trickle of giggles, "Well, if you are that shy, you could wear my lingerie!"

By the time she finished she was out right laughing and darting Naked past him. "Ohhhh, kitten, I don't believe I could fill it out quite as well as you do." His voice was husky as his arm snaked out and scooped her to him. A sharp slap across her rear,

"Shall we get down to business or do we continue playing cat and mouse?" Lilly's long lashes fluttered up as she slides her eyes to meet his. "Patience Harold, I'm well worth taking your time." It was a husky purr he could bear no more.

It was just before dawn when Judge Harold meandered back to his room, glassy eyed tired, in a good way. Opening the door his voice barely above a whisper, "She was well worth taking my time." Lilly laid on the bed smiling.

"I hope all my couples enjoyed the festivities; I know I did." By 9am the coffee shop started filling up.

All seemed quiet but fulfilled. With eye pointed downwards, the men with longer appetites consuming a variety of food from the breakfast bar. With full mouths, everyone agreed to keep the *Key Club* going.

"Always remember this is a sanctuary, free of judgement, fear of retribution, or prying eyes. Problems are too brought to my attention," soothed Judge Harold. "Have a good weekend." As couples left questioning look between partners as they looked about. General things occupied the travel home.

Jack asked Judith, "How are you feeling?" His voice a low concern. "Tired, I don't sleep well outside of my own bed."

Judith came home to dirty dishes, clothes strung everywhere. Looking at Jack shaking her head, "We're home!"

Frank and Roselyn immediately opened the alley, as league practice would start in a few hours. True to word, No one mentioned the event. Only the Reverend waited with bated breath to hear the sorted details of lustful sin.

Opening the confessional, but no one from the group came, just your everyday practitioners. "I took the Lord's name in vain, and even cursed," but not one juicy tidbit for Reverend Thomas to fantasize over.

Pageant tryouts would start at 2pm, another long day of mothers came into the office offering costume ideas for their most perfect prodigy. Reverend Thomas's thoughts drifted as tryouts for the Christmas pageant began. Mother's crowing how their children deserve *starring roles*. He thought of all the sinful acts that had been done the night before. His skin flushed crimson, sweat dripping from his brow.

Calling try out every day, he needed to be alone with his day dreams and a cold shower. Thoughts of young girls primping to be the Christmas queen of the pageant, brought the good Reverend to touching and pleasuring himself feverishly.

A knock at the door deflated his passion. Opening the door a young girl explained, "Momma said you were not feeling well, so she sent me with her homemade soup. Guaranteed to fix whatever is ailing you." "Thank you so much." As he closed the door his thoughts drifted to how this young girl could fix what ails him. "Cold showers just weren't cutting it anymore," he whined.

Judge Harold found himself in private chambers. "Hildi, I have forsaken your memory. I was with Miss Lilly; I need to release my hurt and Lilly helps with that. Please forgive my indiscretions."

A warm touch was felt on Harold's shoulder, "Hildi, I still love you!" With more discussions between husbands & wives it seems the weekend was a successful event.

What could the next event be? A board meeting will help to clarify which direction the next events should take to guide the couples.

Miss Lilly heard whispers of how the women enjoyed the activities of the weekend. Still unsure if they were right in enjoying themselves. Questions filled their minds, *was it ok to enjoy sex without their significant other. What about their children, how will it affect them?*

Because of the newly fallen snow, the next event could be sleigh rides, with an evening of games & drinks before pairing off. Roselyn & Frank are planning for the next event. Staring off out the kitchen window, Roz smiled to herself relishing the touch of the man she paired off with. His touch was soft and gentle.

His tongue tantalized her nether regions. She felt guilty as hell, but boy, did she enjoy herself.

Harold called an emergency board meeting to discuss the next event and to answer questions or concerns. As with any small town, there were those who felt it was wrong and should be drummed out of the Church. These women were truly jealous because they had not been invited to participate. Reverend Thomas helped fan the flames by covering multiple parties in his sermons as a lustful sin.

As the men headed back to work, no one discussed the event, but bosses noticed employees having a bit of pep in their step and better attitudes towards work. A new vigor for the mundane jobs, the men had a new purpose to get the end of their work week. On Friday paychecks are issued & bills are paid. With the Key Club formed, Fridays were a whole new reason to smile.

The ladies were more creative in cooking meals, ready to spice up the family's pallets. There were incoming Phone calls to Judge Harold expressing the enjoyment found by participating in the Key Club. Even the children noticed their parents' happier dispositions.

Calvin, a local sixteen-year-old was on the street corner passing on his street advice. "Hey Calvin, are your parents nicer than normal?" Frank Jr. crowed, "Yes, must be they got some, cause mom & dad are smiling. Hell, mom made us after school snacks and dessert." "Sounds like this Key Club is going to benefit all of us." Cracked Calvin.

"Bet Father Thomas is ticked off, because no one invited his tight ass to the party," cackled Calvin. As more children gathered around Calvin they compared notes on their parents' behavior. "Even Judge Harold seems happier! No reform school was mentioned today"

"Ha! Guess he got his gears greased!" cackled Calvin, "Didn't think his gears worked any more, he's super old after all." "Bet Miss Lilly used a little leather to break his will," choked Frank Jr.

"I hear they are making room for the possibility of future students." "Man," whined Calvin, "That will mess up our time off for hunting." "No worse than the school allowing girls to try out for the rifle club." "If they make it, those girls will compete against us!" "Girls should just stick to cheerleading," cried Frank Jr.

As the kids compare notes Judge Harold announced an immediate board meeting. "Tonight at 7pm our town board will convene." As the board members slowly trudged into the office, Judge Harold greeted all with a broad smile and a twinkle in his eyes.

"So how is everyone feeling about the club's 1st activities?" "According to our factory supervisor's attendance for work is better with an extra spring in their step." "Council woman Summers, how are the ladies feeling about the weekend's events?" "Many were nervous, but they enjoyed themselves."

"Is it true the ladies are more attentive to their families?" Judith began with what she was hearing, "The children have said mothers are being spontaneous in making snacks & desserts."

"So, our children are not complaining. Mothers are also more attentive to their appearances." Lilly jumped in with, "The men are also more attentive to their appearance." "Sounds like all went well, now to plan our next event." "But Reverend Thomas is unhappy because no one chose to confess their sins."

Lilly pipped in, "The ladies auxiliary has already threatened if your apart of the club you are no longer invited to take part in the auxiliary." "I see a town meeting might be needed," growled Harold.

"It's disappointing that our Reverend Thomas would encourage the lack of tolerance amongst our towns people." Council woman Sikes sighed with exasperation, "We knew the town busy bodies would complain." "So, we keep going with the Club or disband it to pacify our anal-retentive Auxiliary members?" After growling several curse words.

Judge Harold bellows, "We will not allow town folk to be bullied for choosing to be in our adult club! Town hall meeting Thursday evening at 7pm. The topic will be the welfare of our town." Slamming the gavel down, Harold bellowed, "We're adjourned." Loud whispers between board members brought concerns.

"Maybe Reverend Thomas should get a suggestion for his Sunday sermon." "Such as?" "The need for tolerance, understanding, and leaving judgement to god."

"It's the same situation as always. If you have money, you rule. Money doesn't produce children to keep our community thriving." Lilly knocked quietly on Harold's private chambers. "Yes! Come in!" growled Harold. "Don't take that tone with me, or I will spank you." Cooed Lilly.

"Sorry Lilly, I just can't believe how narrow minded some of the town folks are." "It's always been this way, Harold. I know they look down their noses at me. They are only nice to me because I know all their dirty little secrets, and I have more money than a King, so they kiss my ass."

"But maybe the towns folk need a wake-up call about our low census for children of school age. Without more people our town will dry up and float away. Farms & factories need able bodied men."

"To many divorces, not enough procreation." Judge Harold nodded in agreement. "That's what needs to be explained at our town hall meeting." Lilly lowered her voice to a near whisper, "Harold, if we don't keep the club going, our population will keep dwindling." "Unfortunately, we are the pilot program so to speak. For the entire tri-county area. The other towns are looking to us to light the way."

Giving Harold a strong embrace, Lilly says, "We have much to think about. Give Hildy my love Harold, I know you speak to her daily." "How did you know I speak to her Lilly?"

 "Because you are a wonderful man Harold, I would expect nothing less than you keeping her close to that mountain of a heart you have."

Smiling weakly, "Lilly you will always be my best friend and confidant." "Right back at you big guy," cooed Lilly. Harold started mumbling to himself, "I'm just doing what's in the towns best interest."

Grabbing the event list, looking through possibilities, thinking about a winter wonderland event. *With the Bever Hilltop Hotel & cabins would provide a private, quiet place for the club. Crackling fireplaces, friendly snowball fights, sleigh rides, and spiced hot buttered rum. Tables filled with aphrodisiacs.* Judge Herald was sweating just at the thought.

Now I need to prepare some visual aids to help explain the town's dire situation. Explaining to his clerks about the statistics needed for the charts along with the size of them.

 So, it couldn't be misinterpreted by the town board, which includes the good Reverend

Thomas. He doesn't need to approve of the Club, just show tolerance to those who choose to be in it. As Harold looks at the charts, he realizes this explanation needs to be idiot proof. Their town depends on it.

Calling Roz, Judge Harold gave her his suggestion about the Bever Hill Hotel & cabins. As Roz listened, she began nodding in agreement suggesting, "I will call Lilly." After a quick call down to the beauty parlor Roz was able to speak to Lilly about Judge Harold's ideas.

Thinking a moment Lilly admitted, "There *would* be more privacy. *But* the idea of making it a home base of sorts, with the local establishments being so close, it makes having **fun** a bit more difficult." After making the arrangements, Lilly called to tell Harold about the Bever being a home base.

"It's unusual, but a damn good idea, Lilly." "So, we will set up for the weekend." "Don't forget the town board meeting." Thursday at 7pm, passing the word out, Lilly was preparing her own words for Reverend Thomas. "Workers seem more willing to work things out rather than argue. Aggressive personalities have softened a bit."

Roz noticed an uptake in family events at the bowling alley. Parents seemed more attentive to children's activities. As Thursday rolled around the members of the board shuffled in.

Seating was designed for all the charts to be in clear view. With the banging of the gavel the meeting began. Judge Harold began, "Seems our church Auxiliary and Reverend Thomas do not understand the meaning of tolerance. This meeting is to show, why the Key club needs to exist." With each chart Judge Harold explained,

"Our town will die without more people, we have less than half of what our census was two years ago. Now that our dire situation has been explained to you, Reverend Thomas, I hope you will talk to your congregation and put an end to this foolishness. I am flat out telling you that I will not tolerate the auxiliary treating the other ladies this way."

"We're here to help our town grow, guide the others, within the tri-state area. Do I make myself clear!?" the buzz was intense within the room as the members whispered. Then Lilly asked to address the meeting. "I have known most of you, your whole lives, that being said I also your secrets that you keep in your pristine closets." "How dare you think you know what's good for this town!"

"The **no mixing** of lineage is absolutely absurd! What gives you the right to judge or look down your noses at anyone! Shall I start **openly discussing the indiscretions** of the

people in ***our town***!?! Most of you have ***NO room*** to talk.!" "This is a very simple equation, Sex equals babies, Children become grown ass adults to function in society, and more people equals more revenue. Since most of the women who complain about the Key Club do not sleep with their husbands anyway, exactly what is your issue?

Because you're *not contributing* in any way to resolve the rising issue. Oh, I remember now, it is about control, and you don't have any, and that pisses you off. Well *maybe* if you spent *more* time with *your mouths full* and *your legs up in the air* you'd have something to smile about, rather than spiteful back biting, goffer digging ditties, you are now."

Chuckling in the corner, Judge Harold was enjoying Reverend Thomas's chastising. "Look; to save this town, it is a necessary evil. So, the next event is already planned, I hope to see many of you there. We are adjourned!"

As board members look back at the census statistics, a chill ran down their spine, this is literally the life and death of the town.

Doc Halloway now understood why he was called to be on staff. This could mean many deliveries, which meant bigger staff. As he drove back to his office, he began to wonder what his father would have thought. When you have practice in the city, such things are not an issue. With what felt like an ice-cold hand on his right shoulder, "Yes dad, I know, I cannot stop analyzing and do my job."

Walking through his dad's cold empty house, he felt a slight breeze on the back of his neck. "Thanks mom, I still miss you every day."

Judith knew there could be an issue with the auxiliary, with Reverend Thomas using his bible as a tool to get rid of the Key Club. Auxiliary ladies tend to be very judgmental, if they had been invited, those ladies would be the first in line with their hands in the key bowl.

Reverend Thomas was not a virtuous man as he would like others to think either. More than half of the town's he preached admitted to questioning his behavior.

Priests take a vow of celibacy; ministers & reverends are allowed to be married. Judith had more questions than answers. Her husband waited up to hear the latest from the town board. Handing Judith a highball, looking into her eyes, Jack asked softly, "How bad was it?" Sitting at the kitchen table, Judith laid out the events of the meeting.

"Harold used charts & statistics to explain the dire straights of the tri-county area. Even with all the charts and visuals, Reverend Thomas is still causing issues. He backs the no tolerance by our church auxiliary." Jack laughed, "Sounds like our Reverend is a bit jealous he wasn't invited."

"They need to pull the stick out of their asses, this club is for the benefit of keeping the town thriving. We're what is referred to as the red flag ship, to light the way." "Is this going to be a problem with the other min9isters of the tri-county area?"

Judith explains, "Not exactly sure but we need the influx of births, or our town will disappear. As well as other towns." "Why can't people understand the majority has no business being involved."

Judith began to understand the religious implications as well as the moral implications.

"But by God our town will disappear! I believe God would understand!" Jack knew they will have to have a private discussion with the Reverand. Bed produced no sleep, Judith's mind filled with questions.

The fact that Judge Harold had to tell them as an order about tolerance is not a good sign. Thinking about the new event, how many will cave under pressure. But the idea of winter fun at the Bever Hill hotel and cabins sounded enticing. Sleigh rides & hot butter rum could grease the wheels for fun.

As Sunday sermon started with a lack of morals causes confusion for the young congregation. "But we need to practice tolerance and understand. It's not just our town that has concerns, our tri-county area has issues as we do." "The congregation agreed to practice tolerance. Our ladies of the auxiliary, I expect a higher standard from you."

A nodding of approval from Judge Harold signified Reverend Thomas is back in his good graces.

Lilly quietly spoke quietly with the key club members about winter sports at the Bever Hill

Hotel & cabins. Ladies admitted their weekend events were the most aerobic workouts they have had in years. Men admitted it made them appreciate their families more. A competition between them and the other men. Proving their sexual prowess.

Lilly then noticed her normal clients were asking for extras, like waxing, new hair colors, even having their nails done. There were visits to the lingerie store, and an uptake in more risky garments. All of these things she reported joyfully to Harold. "Sounds like members have gotten passed the judgement phase. I'll feel better once pregnancies are confirmed."

"I understand Harold, but the fact is pregnancy usually happens when you aren't trying."

"So, we focus on members having fun, the rest will follow in a natural chain of events."

"Maybe you're right Lilly." Harold smiled. "Sex is a natural thing; it should not be a chore, Harold." Smiling Lilly whispered, "We had no problems, did we?" Harold smiled, "No we did not."

Lilly Nodded, "We need to turn up the heat for the couples." "Do you have any suggestions?" Lilly cooed, "You know I am all about a good time." "I think I should check with Doc and make sure he has plenty of tests." Lilly looked at him, "You mean ask if any of the members are using birth control, don't you?"

"Unfortunately, to keep my eyes on all aspects of this project, yes." Thinking a moment, Lilly looked at Harold, "What is it really Harold?" "What happens if our plan doesn't work? We would have to combine town to stay afloat."

"They had to do such things during the depression," Lilly rubbed Harold's shoulders, "This will work, I promise." "I can't not join my Hildi if our town isn't doing ok." "Harold, you aren't ready to meet Hildi yet, you have to much work to do, and she would understand that." "Lilly, I miss my Hildi so much." "Harold, you honored her wishes and let her go. Her pain was excruciating. It took strength and pure love to let her go."

Tear welled up in Harold's eyes, "You know Hildi really liked you, Lilly." Wiping Harold's tears, "Hildi and I, had many wonderful talking about life, love, and you Harold." Lilly whispered, "She loved you so much, you were her world." "Thanks for the support, I need to check in with Doc Halloway."

Dale Halloway was always a good kid, but he always lived in his father's shadow. He was rough on poor Dale. Especially after his mother passed. He went to medical school out of state just to have breathing room. But when Dale got the call, he rushed home to tend to his father and take over his practice.

Dale preferred city life compared to a rural town. He understood the need for the Key Club and procreation. He would be prepared for the onset of pregnancies. Harold took a ride over to Doc Halloway's office. "Hello, what are you doing here Judge Harold?" "Checking in on our status with the Key Club." "I have ordered extra pregnancy tests." "Has anyone in the club asked for birth control?" "Harold, you know I cannot discuss medical records of my patients."

"I understand, how about a simple nod or head shake?" Dale nodded. Judge Harold said, "That's all I needed, thank you."

Shaking his head Dale knew this club was going to expand, with new births. The school would have more students, so more sports. His fee's need to increase. As Judge Harold drove back to his chambers, he felt a pang of both excitement and dread. His job was to ensure his town would thrive, not disappear.

Stopping in at the Bever Hill Hotel to make arrangements for the Key Club. Harold explained he was interested in sleigh rides, dancing, drinks, and a variety of Dish choices on the buffet. As the manager totaled up the costs for Harold, slipping a piece of paper in his direction. Harold retrieved it and signed.

"Seems like our dues are going to have to increase." Harold mumbled. The manager leaned in whispering, "The owner says he give you a discount if this will be your main meeting place." "I will discuss it with the town board." Harold smiled; *things were starting to come together*. A quick call to the board members should be made, in order to take advantage of the discount offered. Grabbing a sandwich, Harold headed back to chambers to make his calls.

"Most everyone agreed to the terms discussed. A few concerns about costs, but in the end, all agreed." Lilly was pleased, "Now we can plan more events with a safe place to meet." With a wink, Lilly cooed, "Now to get down to some baby making. Excitement again filled the air, thoughts of winter fun. Skiing, sleigh rides, slow dancing to set the mood. However, increasing dues could cause issues."

Thinking a moment, Lilly decided to donate financially so there wouldn't be any excuses to close the club. Heading to the local bank, Lilly withdrew 10,000 dollars and headed to the Bever Hill Hotel. Having delivered it to the owner, with a note:

"This should keep us in good graces for a while"

Signed Lilly

Harold was astounded when he received the receipt for Lilly's donation. Harold informed

Lilly's receptionist that he needed to see her. "I bet you do Sir. Trim & a shave today?" "Can we make it the end of the day? So, the clientele is smaller?" "Oh yes Judge, anything you need!"

Hanging up the phone, Harold knew his care would be done by Lilly only. "Judith Summers called asking about rising dues. Harold, are we raising dues or not?" Clearing his throat

"It seems that Miss Lilly donated 10,000 dollars to keeping Bever Hill as our main meeting place."

"Oh, my lord, that was extremely nice of her. The club hasn't off the ground yet, so increasing dues already would be a big turn off." "Once we have a few events under our belts, we can revisit increasing dues Judith." "Are we doing the right thing?" softening his tone,

"They truly don't have another option. If we are successful, the other towns in the tri-state area will follow our model as a guide for their own town." "Understood," cooed Judith, "Are we ready for this weekend's events?"

"I believe we are. Lilly will make sure everyone knows where and what time." Judith says, "I will let Roselynn & Frank know. Anything else?" "Winter wear for outside sports!?"

At 5pm the small town started closing shops, making sure school sports practices were done. The streets quiet with fluffy snowflakes dancing about. Walking quietly, Harold smiled, "This town will survive." Harold let himself into Lilly's salon. Walking towards what looked like a soft glow from the oil lamp.

Taking a few more steps, he realized he was in Lilly's private area. Only a few had ever seen Lilly's office. Harold took a seat at the closed station. Lilly then greeted Harold in a flimsy smock with all her beautiful assets on display. "I understand you are here for a trim & shave?"

"Yes, I am," Croaked Harold. Leaning over to reach for a cape to drape over him. Watching, Harold ends up with a face full of Lilly's voluptuous breasts as she fastened the cape around his neck. Wetting his hair down she accidentally got the front of the smock wet.

Combing his hair, Lilly pulled it up between her fingers and began working on the cut. Thinning hair where it needed to be thinned, styling what needed styling. Harold asks about the donation.

Lilly explained, "No one will enjoy themselves if they must worry about dues. So, I took money out of the equation."

Harold quipped, "Smart thinking, Lilly" As Lilly prepared for the shave, the warm towel had just enough steam to make his skin just right. The warm lather covered his face, Lilly sharpened her straight razor for a perfect shave. With a touch of cologne, Harold admitted his face was as smooth as a baby's bottom.

"I aim to please Harold!" Excusing himself Harold said, "It has been a joy visiting with you Lilly" Lilly smiles whispering,

"Let me know when you're in the mood for full-service treatment." It was a soft husky sound that tantalized his ears like a sweet, promised caress.

As Harold walked the dark town streets, he knew what needed to be done. He was truly fond of Lilly, but she could never replace his beloved Hildi. He knew Hildi would be ok with Lilly, but the town's people would look down upon his choice. So, he would keep his feelings of Lilly put away never to see the light of day.

Lilly was an intracule part of our town, but most looked down their nose at her. Even though her husbands were always rich & politically connected, she was always treated with disdain from the ladies of the auxiliary. But whenever she was needed by those hypocritical women, Lilly always treated them with kindness.

She believed in Karma and eventually they would receive theirs. Arriving at home, Harold poured himself a drink. Pulling off his tie as the housekeeper greeted him with, "Dinner is ready, wash up." Sitting at the table Harold noticed less meat and more vegetables. "What is this all about Janet?" Janet smiles,

"Doc Halloway says your cholesterol is a bit high, so less red meat and more veggies. Here are diet suggestions to help lower cholesterol. This includes alcohol and caffeine."

"Great a new way to frustrate me." "Sir, I am only doing as the doctor said." "I truly understand Janet, but diet food tastes like cardboard." "Plus, you need cardio exercise sir!" "It's fine Janet." Thinking for a moment, his mind wondered to how much cardio he had done with Lilly at the first event.

"I guess I need to speak to Doc Halloway." *Normally there would be statins involved. Will I need medication the rest of my life?* Harold thought. More questions than answers bounced around in Harolds head. He found himself talking out loud with no answers returned. "Hildi, am I falling apart without you?"

A warm light breeze was felt upon his face. "Hildi, I know you are here with me in spirit. You know how much I love you, sometimes I need to be held, but you're not here."

A light movement of air hit the windchimes that Lilly had made for Hildi. "Thank you for the understanding my love." Walking to his bedroom, Janet started a small warm fire for him. Pulling on silk pajamas, Harold snuggled in for the night.

About an hour into his sleep, Harold found himself dreaming he stood at the gates of heaven. God asked, "Do you feel as if you disobeyed the bible over the Key Club?" Understanding the wrath to come, Harold replied,

"My Lord and Father, I stand by my decision to help populate our town. As a Judge I see many come through my courtroom, none wanting to stay married. This was our only option with other towns in the same situation." Just then a thunderous bellow came from above.

Harold jumped out of bed in a cold sweat and ran to his window to see & hear thunder &

snow. Shaking his head, Harold knew he received God's answer.

A soft knock from Janet, "Sir, I brought you some warm milk so you can go back to sleep." "Thank you, Janet,"

"You're welcome, Sir." Quietly shutting his door, Harold grabbed a book to fall asleep with. Taking a drink of warm milk, he recognized nutmeg, cinnamon, and a touch of brandy.

After about 20 and a half pages of the glass of warm milk, Harold had fallen back to sleep.

Janet snuck back into the room and collected the glass half emptied and shut off his alarm so he could sleep in after having a difficult night. At 9a.m, Harold started bellowing,

"Why did you let me sleep late!?!" "Sir, I thought it might be needed after the nightmare." Nodding Harold asked about breakfast. "Vegetarian egg white omelet, turkey bacon, whole wheat toast, and a side of orange juice." "Coffee?" "It's half decaf Sir." "Can't I have 1 cup of regular coffee?"

"It's not on your diet Sir." "Then Doc Halloway and I will be having a conversation I assure you Janet!" "Until I am told otherwise, I am following this diet Sir." "Fine! Then let me eat in peace!"

Janet knew Harold would not be following this diet willingly. Out to run errands for the judge, Janet felt a trip to the library was in order. Looking for recipes the judge would not complain about. She also knew she would have to meet with a nutritionist to find alternatives for his diet. Harold arrived at his office he demanded, "Real coffee, **do not** give me **half assed coffee**!"

While enjoying the aroma of his morning coffee & cigar, Judge Harold was interrupted by Doc Halloway. "I see we aren't following the diet plan."

Letting out a large breath of air, Harold says, "You should have spoken to me first about said diet plan & left my damn coffee alone."

"You would have brushed it off, Harold." Thinking for a moment Harold nodded, "You're probably right. But I'm not sacrificing 1 cup of coffee in the morning. So, what exactly is the problem, Doc?" Smiling Dale put up his test results. "Harold, this is what your numbers should look like for your age, and this number is what your test shows."

"Okey, let's have a look, shall we?" Harold put his reading glasses on and analyzed the results. Grumbling, he asks, "So what do I need to do?" "Your BP is to high and so is your cholesterol. There is medicine for both, but you need to change your diet and exercise. I've noticed you walk to and from work, which is good. I'm willing to allow you 2 cups of caffeinated coffee per day, but decaf for the rest of the day after the initial 2 cups of caffeine.

More vegetables and less red meat. Chicken and fish are better substitutes for red meat. Next your stress levels are through the roof. Delegate some of the club's responsibilities. Get laid, it's great cardio for your heart!"

"Lay off the whiskey, have a glass of wine instead. Harold, if you don't make changes in your lifestyle, you could have a stroke, heart failure, etc. I would like to stop that from happening." Pausing a moment for thoughts, Harold nods, "You win Doc. Please tell Janet we agreed to a compromise." Laughing Dale says, "Janet took my advice hole heartedly I'm guessing."

"Yes, she truly did." Doc Halloway smiles, "Sher is taking care of you like Hildi wanted her to. I will write up new orders, now take these once a day, and try not to miss a dose. If you have any concerning side effects, call me immediately, at home if necessary. Oh, you need to lose 50lbs, slowly though."

"I see you waited until you had one foot out the door to give that bit of information." "The lower your weight, the better it is for your heart, lungs, etc." "Damn, your just full of useful knowledge today."

"I truly want to avoid diet pills, if possible, they are bad on your system." "Ok Doc, I will try my best to follow your instructions. But can I still have my cigars?"

Dale explained, "I would prefer you not, but I will agree to 2 per week, then 1, until finally you have none." "Thank Doc, send me a bill." "It's already in the mail, Harold." Grumbling, Harold admitted to himself that without Hildi it would be difficult. She was his reason for being. Shaking his head, Harold called in his secretary/paralegal, "Yes Sir?"

"I need a large herbal tea with honey." "Excuse me, Did I hear you correctly?"

"Yes, unfortunately Doc Halloway feels my cholesterol is a little high." "So, let me guess, Doc got ahold of your housekeeper." "Boy, was my dinner a surprise. No red meat, I personally find that offensive" Crowed Harold. Duwanna cracked a large smile, "I will assume no more Columbian coffee either." "I'm allowed 2 cups per day otherwise its decaf all day. Plus, cardio exercise."

"Well with the Key Club in full swing that shouldn't be an issue." Duwanna giggled. Coughing Harold expressed, "I'm supposed to be in charge of the Club." "No one would think less of you, Harold."

Changing his formal position, "I walk to work and home so hopefully that will do the trick."

"Anything else before I run out to ger your herbal tea?" coughed Duwanna. "Knock it off or I will find you something to work on." "Yes Sir." Duwanna giggled.

"Ugh, this will be a nightmare." Complained Harold. Sitting at his massive desk Hildi had made for him as a graduation gift after law school. There has been sweat and blood and tears as Harold toiled over his rulings.

Harold always thought long and hard before making decisions that affect the lives of his constituents. A buzzing come from Duwanna's desk. Harold hit the button blinking red, "Good morning, how may I help you?" Lilly squealed, "Harold, why are you answering your own phone!?!" "Duwanna is running errands, and I asked her to bring me a herbal tea with honey." Lilly quietly asked, "Harold, are you ill?"

"No, my cholesterol is just a bit high." He grumbled and explained his new diet and exercise plan. Lilly smiled through the phone, "I can take care of you Harold. Hildi wouldn't want you not getting taken care of."

Harold knew she truly meant the offer to be heart felt. But he was still a sitting judge as well as the mayor. So, his behavior needed to be beyond reproach.

Lilly said, "I will contact Janet to discuss tastier dinner options for you. I will also assume your blood pressure was a bit high. I'll help with your cardio." She giggled. "Thank you, Lilly, everything is set up for this weekend?" "Yes sir, arrangements have been made." "Do we all drive up separately?" asked Lilly. "Maybe after we get a few events under our belt. Then maybe they will carpool." "Get rested up Harold, we will have fun this weekend."

Shaking his head he admitted that he looks forward to the time spent with Lillian. They shared a lot of history, including presiding over all her weddings. Hildi was also close to Lilly. The friendship evolved since they were all children.

Most of the town's folk have descendants that started the township.

Harold's father was the first sitting judge for their county seat. Most have a stake in the town. So, their idea of the Key Club became necessary. As Duwanna arrived, she said, "Herbal tea has so many varieties." "Which one will give me a boost?"

"I went for ginseng, I hope it works like coffee." "It may take awhile for you to get used to it. After a few weeks you should notice a difference." "But 2 cigars a week will kill me! I need those babies! Thank God Doc Halloway didn't take them completely." "But he will, maybe you should consider hard candy or toothpicks, just for chewing on." "Maybe, I will see how this works first."

Duwanna cooed, "Doc Halloway just doesn't want you to stroke out or have a heart attack. If you keep this shit up, you're going to need a

pacemaker. Harold, I have been here since you opened your practice. The town looks up to you, but honestly if you don't concentrate on your health, the whole plan you developed to save our town will be moot if you die."
"Damn it, I hate it when you're right."

"Now get your ass behind that desk, drink your tea, and review the cases you need to rule on. You will have a walk around town at noon. The more you move the better off you are." "Yes mom!" Cracked Harold. "Well, if you won't listen, I will invite the women of auxiliary to take care of you."

"Christ, No, I will follow Doc's orders." "I brought you soup and salad for lunch." Getting himself simi comfortable to go through cases and give his ruling.

The ginseng tea seemed to help his motivation, *maybe this wouldn't be so bad after all.* The case at the bottom of the pile bothered him. Calling the Family Social

Services worker, he knew this would not be a popular rule.

*The boy needed to be evaluated for a diagnosis. Doc Halloway suggested a psychiatric evaluation. A classification would at least give the school an idea of how to better handle his situation. He's gifted in math & science, history pertaining to strategic tactical battle plans he excelled in. English was difficult as he was dyslexic. His parents don't want him being labeled as **retarded** as children are want to do, and sometimes other adults. His physical aggressiveness has teachers concerned.*

These were the cases Harold wished he didn't have to preside over.

Our beloved town is known for its open arms, until it's not, when you're not perfect or don't fit their idea of perfection. The lady of the auxiliary said the boy was possessed.

Reverend Thomas was always requesting prayers for the boy. GAWD has a plan even if we don't understand!

Shaking the cobwebs of sarcasm and disdain from his mind, Harold started to prepare for his long walk home. Pulling up his collar he went to open the door and discovered Lilly waiting to greet him. "Miss Lilly, to what do I owe this pleasant surprise?" "I thought I would walk with you. I'm sure you have plenty of things to talk about." "You know me so well, Miss Lilly." "So, how was your day?" "I went over pending cases and gave rulings."

Lilly pouted, "I know you were concerned about the boy." "I believe this needs a professional diagnosis; his problems need better understanding if he's to get any form of positive assistance. Especially for his family."

"That sounds like a solid decision." "Lilly if I was wrong would you tell me?"

"Harold, if I thoughts for a second you were wrong about anything, I would tell you. I believe in the truth no matter how much it hurts." "So, are you ready for Bever Hill, Lilly?" "Always, I think a weekend is what these couples need." "And I will be by your side at all the events." Lilly squeezed his hand. As they opened the door Janet greeted them with a drink and notice that dinner would be ready in about 30 minutes.

Handing Lilly, the list of dietary changes, reading his test scores and going through changes for exercise. Lilly brought a book of recipes she received for her second husband's health.

Janet gave Lilly a questioning look. With a faint smile she explained, "My second husband, Claude, had the same issues, but he didn't heed Doc Halloway's advice. Six months later he had a heart attack that he didn't recover from. So, I intend to care for Harold, I'm not ready for him to pass." Smiling Lilly whispered, "You feed him, I will be in charge of his exercise." Janet winks, "Got it."

Janet peeked around the corner, "No more bourbon, get washed up."

Shaking his head, "Darn women are still telling me what to do!"

Pulling out Lilly's chair, Harold showed his perfectly polished manners. Looking to the place his Hildi sat, he gave a nod to her empty chair. Janet served Salmon with boysenberry sauce, steamed Brussel sprouts, and herbal rice.

Harold rolled his eyes but tried the salmon, after a few bites he decided it wasn't that bad. But dessert was fruited Jello.

Janet cleaned up the kitchen, then offered Lilly a ride back to her shop. "I just like that Harold wasn't alone with his thoughts."

In his home office, Harold wandered, looking at his & Hildi's wedding photos. *He was so young and idealistic, she was so beautiful with her long chestnut hair, petite figure, and penetrating hazel gaze. One had to but look into her eyes, you became mesmerized and did what you were told.*

She could talk down a raging hippo and keep it calm. Harold envied that about her. Her gentle demeanor helped with clients. Harold ambled over to the closet pulling out a silk nightgown, holding it close to his face, and inhaling deeply. The scent alone brought memories to the forefront of his mind.

Putting the garment back, Harold got into bed for the night. As he started dozing off a sudden wave of cold air enveloped him. "It's not time for you to join me. You still have so many things left to do. Our town's folk need your strength to keep it alive. Stick to the plan, take help where you need it, and give our beloved town life again. Good night my love."

Harold hugged Hildi's pillow tight, "I love you Hildi, good night." A deep sleep enveloped Harold, Knowing Hildi believes in him is what he needs to carry on.

At many of the other homes whispers of Judge Harolds health circulated. Frank announces, "We all need to take better care of ourselves. I'm sure Doc Halloway would give us all the same advice." Roz fully admitted to having a pence to fried salty foods. "Well to produce quality offspring, we should probably keep bad habits at a minimum, but we enjoy a glass of wine."

Roz adds, "Probably more like, no cigarettes, cigars, whiskey, fried foods, coffee, etc. Salt is a big thing too." "Do you think Harold will be ok?" "I don't believe he has a choice, this town counts on him." "We do count on him quite a bit." Admitted Roz. "So have you been advised of our event?" asked Frank. "Yes," Roz gave a skip across her kitchen.

"Winter sports at Bever Hill Hotel & Cabins." Cooed Roz. "I hear Lilly put down $10k on the Bever Hill to be our official meeting place." "It was either that or dues would have increased exponentially." "Lilly admitted that if they can't afford the dues, it defeats the purpose of the Key Club."

"Obviously we should re-imburse Lilly." Frank giggled. "Seems she is concerned with people enjoying themselves." Roz asked, "Will Lilly take over if Harold has to step down?" Frank laughed,

"Lilly could run this town with one hand tied behind her back." Roz smiled, "The lady is truly connected. I offered to make Harold some Minestrone soup so Janet can have a break."

"Will the other ladies follow suite?" "Oh yes, the man won't know what hit him, but he'll know how much he's loved." "I'm sure he will absolutely know he is cared for." "Duwanna has the office covered, Janet and Lilly have food covered, and Lilly is taking care of his exercise regiment as well." Roz laughed, "Healthy I bet she is!"

"It's not advisable to piss off your coach. Miss Lilly could make it hurt." "In her defense, I believe pain & pleasure could be attributed to exercise." "I refuse to entertain that concept." Roz smiled. The same discussions were taking place all over town. Concerns about Judge Harold only flamed the fire of the auxiliary. They were convinced GOD was punishing Harold.

Reverend Thomas said, "God is a fair and loving God. Harolds health comes with age and nothing more or less."

He was trying to defuse the rumor mill, but they may need to hear from Doc Halloway. "Just what's needed more B.S about the Key Club." The closer to Friday, the buzz in town sounded like bees in a Hive. The adults stop in for a trim & wax, ladies quietly shopping for lingerie two towns over.

Men started lifting weights. Roz told everyone, "Friday night 7pm at Bever Hill. Pack for over Night, home in time for Saturday evening bowling league, with Sunday morning service." Even the men broke out their tight-fitting jeans, cologne filled everyone's nostrils.

Judith Summers helped with the arrangements for all the babysitters. Recreations for the kids to stay occupied.

Calvin and his buddies were planning for a party themselves. Supervisor is any 18yr old they can find. Unfortunately, parents were notified of the party plans. Frank & Roz offered the bowling alley for the older kids to use.

Reverend Thomas offered his services as chaperon. Judith smirked, "Now that is help that is appreciated." Quietly couples loaded overnight bags into cars and made the trip to Bever Hill. Which seemed to go at a snail's pace. Once everyone arrived, Harold welcomed all the couples. "Seems we have sleighrides, night skiing, buttered rum, and dancing till dawn. There are delicious treats on the tables, after a drink or two you're free to try any of the ongoing events."

Landing in the arms of your partners atop of soft snow was the right amount of fun needed for the evening events. Watching people starting to split off, Lilly felt the time was near to put keys in the bowl.

As before the ladies face forward while grabbing a key. Lilly had party favors put in each room. Chocolate and/or fruits to tingle the taste buds. Laughing, holding a can of whipped cream, "This can be fun!"

The halls became a sound of happy adult moans of pleasure, filling the air. Judge Harold stayed in his room. Softly Lilly knocked on Harolds door, "Are you ok Harold?" "Yes, Lilly I have to admit that I'm afraid of physical exertions." "I will help if you would like." "That is very considerate of you." "We can take it slowly, that way if you get overly excited, you can pull back and rest a bit."

After some coaxing, Lilly got Harold to relax. Once he realized his heart wasn't going to explode, he began to enjoy Lilly's special lessons. He could now except the changes in his health, it doesn't make him less of a man.

Harold decided the men needed a rec-center, just running a basketball around the court could help the heart. Watching couples arriving for breakfast, just as fast as they arrived, they headed out for some skiing before heading home.

Arriving home, Judith was surprised the kids did chores and cleaned the house. "Christ who crashed the car?" "What?" asked Jack. "You know damn well if they willingly do chores they messed up. Or its report card time again." "Maybe they're just being considerate." Frank laughed. "I guess we go looking for the darn damage." Roz said, "It's too quiet not a good sign."

Walking the perimeter of the house, Frank found nothing amiss. As Roz checked the bedrooms, even the attic, everything was as it should have been. Frank headed to the bowling alley, figuring their party got out of hand. Flipping on the lights, Frank began exploring the kitchen. The dishes were done but not put away.

Judith came in flustered, "Where the hell are my children? My house is clean, but no one is home."

"They left a note saying Reverend Thomas asked them to help with the Pageant decorations." Heading toward the church, Judith had a scowl across her face. Opening the rectory doors, Roz quipped, "They must be practicing with the choir." Listening Roz & Judith could hear the ladies of the auxiliary making demands and complaining about lack of parent supervision. Judith announced her presence by reminding the kids about league practice tonight.

The ladies of the auxiliary took Snipes at Roz & Judith because the children were left unattended. "If you're going to throw insults, get your stories straight, the kids had a party at the bowling alley where Reverend Thomas chaperoned.

They did their chores, cleaned up the bowling alley, and it seems to me that our older children handled their responsibilities well. Or do you not agree?"

Calvin gave his opinion, "Look our parents are *allowed* to have fun. *My* parents *work fucking hard*, so back off. As for you ladies, the auxiliary was not created as a pulpit so you can look down your noses at those who choose to participate in the Key Club." "I believe Judge Harold has already spoken about tolerance. So let us not judge, lest Yee be judged accordingly."

Harold stood outside listening to the conversation. Sounds like our ladies have found a voice. The fact that Calvin, a teenager, understood parents needed a break showed potential leadership qualities. Harold would think long and hard before saying anything.

As the Judge, Harold became lost in thought, his vision of a boarded-up town with dirty windows and no people just wouldn't do. He thought about how to change that vision.

New blood is a must to bring our town back to the glory it once was. Heading back to his office to make notes on the progression of events. Thinking of a roller-skating party for the adults, or a costume party, ideas danced about his head, and he thought about how gentle Lilly had been easing him into cardio exercises.

He had always had a soft spot for Lilly, even in high school. Even though she was physically attractive, she was smart, the first female to serve on the debate team. She was also the first female to lead the rifle club to victory.

Lilly had always been a force to recon with. Plus she ran Student council, believed that because her family was poor that she needed to do better in scholastics.

Knowing her family would need her help with bills and survival. Lilly tested out of three classes so she could take cosmetology and have the skills to support her family. She began helping the local beauty shop clean up, but she got hands on training to help get her license. Her first job was caring for the elderly though. A lady down the street at the tender age of 9.

Always bringing her wages home to her parents. By 15 Lilly had 2 jobs, 1 at the soda fountain at the drug store, and at the beauty salon. With a combination paycheck, Lilly bought her sisters each a new dress, and the younger ones got candy. Lilly had planned on buying herself a new dress! Knowing how hard she had worked, the owner of the dry goods store changed prices so Lilly could have a new dress.

With age comes knowledge, learning you need to be everything for your clients.

Dedicated to her clients, she did things like getting up at 4am to make sure they looked perfect for an event. This work ethic compounded with the drive to succeed only advanced her career. This place is important to Lilly, and she is not above using her own money to keep her hometown afloat.

 Hildi was raised with money but had always felt at home with Lilly's family. She was always close to them. This is the stock our town was based on. Making notes, Harold started fleshing out a town family tree. Maybe it will help or town remember how it got started.

Lilly peeked in, "How are you doing today?" "I'm fine. I decided to make a town family tree as a reminder of what our town stood for." Lilly cooed, "You know this is because they weren't invited." Harold grumbled, "They are to frigid to have any basis of fun." "So has all the club members checked in?"

"Yes, it was a success." "Does that mean we start planning the next one?" "Let's try a costume party, themed for Christmas." "Oh, I like men in tights Howard." Harold laughed aloud, "I bet you do."

"You and I could play Mr. & Mrs. Clause, Harold." Harold laughed, "Now that sounds like fun." "Well, I do have the belly to go with it. The ladies will want to make their own costumes, and the men will be thrilled." Cackled Harold.

"You would be surprised at the men who cross dress," smiles Lilly. "I will take your word for it." Cracked Harold. "So how long before we see results?" Lilly thought a moment and smiled explaining, "That depends, there are many factors for conception." "How are they in their cycles, or do they need some rejuvenation, you know the blue pill." Lilly shrugged, "Depends on how many cobwebs need knocked off."

"Porn doesn't always cause excitement, especially with women. Women like to have all the attention, and the treatment. Women have romanticized views on sex."

"Whereas men treat it like a job or a conquest" Harold understood the dance between male and females. 'Pass around this weekend's Christmas costume party invites." "Yes sir," giggled Lilly. After she left, Harold became lost in thought. He had not appreciated all the planning for conception.

Thinking back, he and Hildi had thought of having children, but they always seemed busy, and time slipped away. By the time they started to prepare for children, Hildi was diagnosed with an aneurysm. So, they concentrated on Hildi getting better.

Harold decided that children would not be a part of their future. As Harold looked out on to the courthouse square the town was decorating for the holidays. Blinging lights throughout the town. Stores filled their windows with the latest clothing and toys. The hunting supply store brought out their finest rifles to tempt wives who had no idea what to buy f their men.

The church was in full on holiday mode, with choir practice, Christmas music, all while the pageant directed rehearsed lines. The air filled with sound. Ladies of the auxiliary taking measurements for costumes as the children had grown quite a bit since the previous year. Even Lilly passed out the information about the new event. Ladies began designing their elf costumes, men dressed as Santa,

Refreshments will be fresh eggnog with a splash of rum, treats of every kind to be enjoyed, the trees & mistletoe to be hung. Each room would have fun toys to play games with. Doc Halloway admitted there were a few cases of the flu but that was to be expected.

Harold even broke out his favorite sheet music for singing around the Baby Grand Piano. Once the eggnog started flowing there would be singing. Plans were subject to change but all had gone well so far. As Harold thought about the holiday parties, Hildi's soft whisper rang in his ears,

"They were always the talk of the tri-county area. All were invited, whether they were blue collar, poor, or well off. The parties for the children, with gifts galore, and cards for the parents to spend on a family Christmas." Harold couldn't help but smile.

He as reminded of how much he loved his hometown and why he could never live anywhere else. Lilly looked into Harold's eyes, "Memories, Harold?" she asked. A sad smile told her all she needed to know.

She knew in her heart that Harold loved her, but his love for Hildi will always be foremost in his heart. Understanding her place with Harold will always be. The scandal would be enormous. The towns' people would not accept it. Coming back to reality, "Harold, I picked up your Santa suit from the cleaners."

"Thank you, Lilly!" "So how goes the ward of the month?" "I'm sure we will have a house full." "Good I went over to the fun shop, outside of our town, for toys & treats." Covering his face, Harold spread his fingers and peeks through them at Lilly, "Do I want to know?" "I think some maybe against the law," Lilly giggled.

"Just what I need, our ladies of the auxiliary will stir up more shit, Lilly." "Well, if they got some maybe they would not be so judgmental." "I'm pretty sure their husbands would like to join the Key Club, but their wives for bid it, for fear they might find someone else."

Lilly cracked, "If those women were more attentive, and not duty bound, 2 x a month their husbands might crack a smile." "Jesus Christ, control is a big issue with those women." "So, who do you think the wisemen will be this year?"

"Not sure, but I found a new type of candy cane," Giggled Lilly. Harold gave Lilly a big bear hug and whispered, "You're such a naughty girl." With a wink and grin Lilly whispered, "Just for you, Harold." As he walked around the town to find lunch, Harold noticed a hum around town. People seemed content and relaxed; this was how town life should be.

Delivery mail, Sidney the local postmaster stopped Harold. "What's the problem Sidney?" "I have a whole storeroom filled with packages for Miss Lilly, but we don't have enough people to deliver them." Thinking a minute, Harold suggested, "We have the old Sleigh. It should get the job done, and it's nostalgic." "But." Whined Sidney, "Those presents are for all the children."

"So, ask Calvin to help. He could use the exercise, plus if you throw the older kids some money, you will have all the help you need. Tell them to see me for payment. Damn I'm hungry!" Harold exclaimed as he walked into the local eatery. The waitress nodded to him. Taking a seat in the back, the waitress brought him a menu with circled items for his new diet.

Looking a bit discouraged, Harold said, "Seafood bisque, a green salad, and green tea with lemon." Smiling the waitress added, "We will add a little extra to your salad.

We can't have you blowing away now, can we?" "Smart ass," he growled. "No Harold, we love you so we will help you reach those health goals"

Letting out a sigh, Harold knew the waitress truly meant the town loved him, his father along with the others started this town. Through blood, sweat, and tears the town grew. Always proud of the small town welcoming new travelers and families. Harold headed back to his office; he took the long way just to help with cardio activity. Just then a yell spun Harold around to see where it came from.

Calvin and the boys were yelling, "Thanks for recommending us! We'll be over later!" Nodding, Harold knew he made their day. Extra money was hard to come by. Shaking off the cold, Harold entered the outer office. His secretary said, "You have some interesting messages." "Explain," bellowed Harold.

"Seems some of your divorce cases have asked to finalize their cases. Seems the Key Club has given them fresh eyes on how much they love their spouse." Shaking his head, Harold explained, "I will adjourn it until couples decide the expected outcome."

Duwanna announced, "We have 5 couples that are reconsidering the status of their marriage. Even some that were looking at separation are looking into therapy." Herold laughed aloud, "Guess they just needed a little competition to give them renewed interests in their wives. If anyone calls, we will adjourn proceedings, pending the need for a dissolution of their domestic union."

"Janet called, she has an appointment out of town, your dinner will be ready for the oven when you arrive home, with specific instructions." "I see," smiled Harold. "No, I will be over to make sure you eat. There will be no scotch, cigars, or pork rinds for dinner!" "Ha!" Snorted Harold,

"Lilly will be over after she closes shop." Grumbling, "Damn doctors worry to much." "But judge, you set the example for the rest of the town."

"Stop reminding me of that! When do I get to just e myself!?!" "Only with me Harold!" Standing behind him was Lilly smiling brightly. "Are you behind this?" Letting out a sign, "Harold, you might as well reconcile yourself to the fact we love you and will try to take care of you as Hildi would have expected of us. You are only allowed to die of old age!"

"Understood," snickered Harold. Heading to his office, Lilly was on his heels. "What?"

asked Harold. "Nothing, I was just checking on you." "I had lunch." Smiling Lilly spoke, "I know. I spoke with the waitress on adding extras to the salad and extra crackers for soup. Now before you start Bitchin, listen."

"You are a big guy, so after a bit of research, I figured portion sizes are crucial for weight loss and cholesterol control. So I discovered how we can add things to keep you fuller longer. So, I had them make you a grazing bowl, it will have different nuts, granola, and maybe little bits of dark chocolate." Smiling at Lilly, Harold asked, "Am I to assume Doc Halloway approved of this?" "Yes, he explained that nuts have good fats, to get rid of the bad ones."

Thinking for a moment, Harold softened his posture, speaking softly, "You really care, don't you?" "Yes Harold, I love you, your loss would devastate me." "But I would never disgrace Hildi's memory. Let's discuss the preparations for the weekend." "Thanks for getting the boys to deliver the presents." "Thinking about using the sleigh to deliver the presents for the kids." Lilly smiled. "That seems like a novel idea," quipped Harold.

"I need to share the adult party plans at the board meeting." "How about I write up a flyer," smiled Lilly. "Give some to Roz, she can pass them out at the bowling alley." 'Anything from Doc Halloway?" "He did say flu was going around." Lilly questioned, "Doesn't pregnancy symptoms start out like the flu?" "Maybe a call to nurse Kelly to see how many are experiencing flu symptoms." "Is it possible already?" Lilly asked. Harold scrunched his nose and forehead up, "This is a subject I do not have experience in Lilly." "Okay, I will speak with Roz & Judith."

Dialing 9 on the keypad to dial the outside line, Lilly made the arrangements to meet with the ladies at the coffee shop. Duwanna popped in with, "You have a meeting with the D.A. and the public defender." "Yes, I remember." Harold shook his head; petty criminals appear with more vigor during the holidays.

Arriving on time, Lilly noticed there were more patrons for the meeting. Greeting Roz & Judith, Lilly ordered coffee. "So, here are the plans for our weekend event." Browsing the list Roz comments on the party for the children. "Lilly, it's not your responsibility to throw the children a party." Smiling Lilly explains, "It's because I can't have children of my own, I consider the town's children as my children." Judith interjected, "You have such a big heart." Lilly smiled, "At least my heart & my chest is the same size." Laughing hard tears rolled down their cheeks. Roz then asked, "How is our big guy handling his restrictions?" "Grumbling at every turn, but he's trying to follow Doc Halloway's advice." "Speaking of the Doc, seems there's a flu going around, what are the chances that it's pregnancies instead?"

"Not sure," replied Roz, "But the symptoms are the same as the flu." Judith announced, "It's a bit early in, but still plausible."

"What happens if all the ladies are due at the same time?" "Train as midwives I guess," answered Lilly. "Ah, maybe we could get some residence to do their training hands on." Judith thought for a moment, "Maybe if they got college credit for it we would have more interests?" "That's totally doable, plus a regular GP (general practice) resident for things like sports physicals." "Now we are rolling with ideas," cracked Judith.

"I will mention it at the board meeting," Judith quipped. "So, now down to the nitty gritty, how do you believe the club is going since we have had a couple of events?" Roz spoke up, "I believe it is helping the couples regain some spark in their home lives." Judith cracked, "More attention is always welcome." Lilly asked, "How are the men feeling about the club?" "From what I have observed, at the bowling alley, the men are different now." Explained Roz,

"It used to be we would have to throw them out at closing time. Not so much anymore. More couples are bowling together and having fun."

"That is a very good sign," giggled Lilly. "We just must get through the Christmas Pageant, then things should calm down. By Valentines Day we should have some verified pregnancies. Fall babies are nice, like changing of seasons."

Heading back to the bowling alley, Judith asked Roz, "What do you really think?" Roz thought for a moment, "People seem to be happier, that seems to be factual. What concerns me is what happens when they are pregnant? I know we all agreed to raise them as a community, but how do we explain this to the children we already have? Will they be accepted or treated like pariahs by the others?"

"Eventually our teenagers will ask the hard questions. Seems like something that should be brought up at the board meeting." "I don't believe the children will be the biggest problem, but the busy body auxiliary will be very intolerant and telling the kids *their* version of our towns problems." "Ah shit!" Cried Judith.

"The more we talk about it the more concerns get raised." "So, we handle it one day at a time."

"Did you hear about the flu bug hitting some of our members?" Judith thought for a moment with a questioning look firmly upon her face. "Flu bug?" With the board meeting set for Thursday to prepare for their Christmas event. Roz had brought up how the children would be treated. Which was brought up before. With assurance that everyone would be treated the same.

Roz also knew that the auxiliary would have their say. Excited for the Christmas event, the Key Club would be in full swing. Dancing & drinks would make for a nice evening. No kids screaming MOM. Roz acknowledged, "It's nice to be away from the kids."

Judge Harold sent out the word that he wanted to bring the meeting to order tonight, in case there were any issues to discuss. As Judith ran through her front door, she headed for the kitchen, pulling out the casserole to be put in the oven. "Jack there's a meeting tonight!" Judith yelled as she prepared to leave. "So, I serve dinner?" "No but you may have bed & bath duty, and don't forget to check homework!"

The kids are getting a little lax the closer Christmas vacation comes. As the kids filed through the door, making a beeline to the bridge for snacks. Judith asked, "How was school?" a growl from the oldest child,

"The teachers want to give us a big ass project for our vacation." Judith cracked, "Let me guess, you do not agree." "Ma, it's supposed to be a vacation. Not indentured servitude. We do not attend school so the teachers can have a vacation." "I never realized you felt like this," Judith replied.

"Mom, look, I know college will be a lot of work, but our high school doesn't give you a break. How about the kids that have jobs or must work on a farm? Or hunting to feed families?" "Now I understand," Smiled Judith. "Even when some of our class will never get to experience college due to lack of finances." Jack had been listening at the kitchen door.

Heading to his room for homework. "Judith, it sounds like our son is concerned about his fellow students." "I guess the idea of a winter project was displeasing."

"The issue is keeping them busy. Idle hands are the devil's plaything, I believe is the saying. Keeping them busy keeps them out of trouble." "So, what's the meeting about?" "The treatment of children after conception. Roz figures the auxiliary will be the ones to tell the children about their lineage."

"Yeah, those nosey broads will cause problems." "Jack, they could blow our plans right out of the water." He shook his head," Not if Judge Harold has his way." "The key to keeping this plan alive is centered around Reverend

Thomas, because if he shows tolerance, those busy body bitches won't have a leg to stand on." "Let's hope you can both control the aftermath." "But Jack, those women are so jealous, sabotaging the plans would be the ultimate form of control and we both know they are like snakes lying in wait."

Changing for the meeting, Judith began thinking about what Calvin had said. He was growing up so fast, but he was right about the kids, about having to help support the families already as children. Smiling Judith thought about her son becoming senator or some other government official. "We never thought how our plan could affect the children."

Peeking into Cal's room, "Hey, would you wanna write down your concerns and I will bring them up at the meeting?" "Really Mom!?!" "You have valid points that I don't believe should be ignored."

He quickly pulled a sheet of paper out and wrote down the concerns, as he could see them, and handed them to Judith. "I was hoping that you would listen Mom, thank you.

Just because we're kids doesn't mean our views are not valid." Calvin hugged his mother tight. "Thank you for always listening."

Judith giggled, hugging him tightly in a bear hug, "I'm always going to lend you my ears and listen." "Smart ass," Cracked Calvin. "Now I know where I get my attitude from." Judith smiled, "You get your blue eyes from your father." "I know mom." Heading out the door, Judith thought, *we have raised a good man, but he will always be my little boy.*

Driving through town, Judith smiled looking at the blinking lights with each pole decorated. This was her home and she was proud to live here. Pulling in, Judith noticed she was the first to arrive. Walking through the corridor, she nodded to Duwanna.

Harold invited her to join him in the chambers. "I hear there are questions." "Yes, but Calvin wrote me a list of things plaguing the children in the high school." Her proud smile couldn't be broader as she handed

Harold the list. As he read the list a smile spread broadly across his face as well. "Seems your boy is going to replace me with these aspirations. He is quite a speaker. So, Judith, it also seems you and Roz had a discussion." "Yeah, we have concerns about the children, and how they are treated."

Harold explained, "I'll handle it." "It's just, you know how the auxiliary women are."

As more board members arrived, there was a low buzz filling the room. Harold brought the meeting to order. Covering the normal list of issues. Then Harold decided to read Calvin's list to everyone. As they listened there were nods in agreement.

"So, as I understand we are still having intolerance issues. Reverend Thomas, I understand you have stepped in and handled it. Thank you for that.

Now, if an auxiliary person, in the future, decides that telling the children about their lineage, I will personally fine you each and every time you do so, until you are so poor as the others you look down your noses at. Do I make myself clear on this issue?"

"But – but" "No, I have heard enough of your petty jealousy. We are trying to save our beloved town, and the tri-county area. If you won't be apart of the solution, then you're choosing to be a problem, and it will not be tolerated. You will keep quiet, or you will give every penny you can rub together until you have nothing left to speak about."

"Now our Christmas event is scheduled for this weekend. Costumes and plenty of fun could be for ALL!" Lilly announced her presence by announcing, "Their will be new toys put in each room. A full Buffet, Winter sports, and there is a piano for Christmas carols!" "We are adjourned!"

The buzz was so loud as they filed out of the meeting room. "Who does he think he is!?!"

"He's the town Justice & Mayor" Reverend Thomas offered, "I suggest we remember that in the future ladies."

Roz & Judith seemed relieved that Harold was taking no crap from those snot-nosed ladies. On his way out, Harold called Doc Halloway, "Hey Dale, What's the status on that Flu bug going around?" "Just the nausea, lightheaded, puki, and in general blah." "Anything else I should know about?"

"I will sneak in pregnancy tests while treating for the flu." "But will you keep me appraised?" "I will let you know if there is a confirmed pregnancy, Harold." "Thanks Doc." "Oh by the way, no I'm not taking you off the healthy diet." "You can't blame a guy for trying!" Laughed Harold.

As Friday rolled in, the kids were planning a roller-skating party at the roller rink. Pizza, fries, and munchies, how could you ask for more.

Roz finished packing for the overnight event. Checking the fridge and cupboards for quick snacks. "Mom did you remember…" "Yes soda is in cases on the back Porch!"

"Calvin be nice to the smaller children please." As she walked by, Roz put some cash in Calvin's hand. "What's this for Mom?" "I'm proud of you. Even Harold was impressed with your list of concerns." Calvin laughed, "I love you, have fun mom, now get out."

As the adults headed to Bever Hill. Pulling into the parking lot, Roz could hear the piano, in full boogie mode. Drinks were available! Lilly put a hand on Roz's shoulder, "I have the perfect costume for you." Lifting a brow, Roz questioned Lilly's choice. Once costumes were passed out the fun could begin.

The room was filled with tin soldiers, dolls, and elves. Just then the sound of Sleigh bells interrupted the chatter. Mr. &Mrs. Clause had Arrived.

Lilly passed presents out, along with plenty of mistletoe. Watching the buffet dwindle, it was time!

Facing front, the ladies grabbed a key and headed upstairs. Lilly explained she would be available for questions about the toys. Lilly monitored and walked through the halls until she was sure everything was in good hands. Smiling at Harold, Lilly whispered, "Are you ready for your Christmas surprise? I brought Candy canes."

Standing under a sprig of mistletoe, Harold received the 1st of several kisses. Pressing the voluptuous breasts of her costume against his arm & chest. Harold only uttered a low gasp. *This is going to be the best Christmas present ever,* Harold thought. "Here Harold, these are special."

Looking at it was supposed to be the face of Pinocchio. But when Harold discovered what the surprise was, he became even more excited. A type of excitement, promise of sorts that is unspoken but it hangs there like a tantalizing taste you didn't know you craved, the gift of everlasting wood much like Pinocchio's nose.

Lilly's gifts were indeed inspirational throughout the night. The following morning during the breakfast buffet, Bill

Emerson suggested trying an entire weekend of the next event. "Maybe if everyone agrees" Lilly took it upon herself to go table to table to see how many agreed with the idea and collected a head count for the full weekend offer.

Heading home always seemed like it passed too fast. No warmth for afterglow. On Sunday

Doc Halloway was called as some of the ladies were not feeling their best. By Wednesday Doc

Halloway's waiting room was filled with women all complaining about having the flu. But Urine tests state that is a lie.

Epilog

What started as the flu bug quickly showed to be a flood of pregnancies. It wasn't that it hadn't been expected to happen, that was the entire idea as it started, but all at once. How does a small community deal with mass births and keep certain elements from coming to light down the road as children grow into adults?

Donna Emerich

www.ingramcontent.com/pod-product-compliance
Lightning Source LLC
Chambersburg PA
CBHW020939090426
42736CB00010B/1198